Gold Bee

Crab Orchard Series in Poetry
OPEN COMPETITION AWARD

Gold Bee

poems by BRUCE BOND

Crab Orchard Review &
Southern Illinois University Press • Carbondale

Southern Illinois University Press
www.siupress.com

Printed in the United States of America

19 18 17 16   4 3 2 1

The Crab Orchard Series in Poetry is a joint publishing venture of
Southern Illinois University Press and *Crab Orchard Review*. This
series has been made possible by the generous support of the Office
of the President of Southern Illinois University and the Office of the
Vice Chancellor for Academic Affairs and Provost at Southern Illinois
University Carbondale.

Editor of the Crab Orchard Series in Poetry: Jon Tribble
Judge for the 2015 Open Competition Award: Cyrus Cassells

Cover illustration: *Tears of Ra* by Stephanie Wilde, cropped

Library of Congress Cataloging-in-Publication Data
Names: Bond, Bruce, 1954– author.
Title: Gold bee / Bruce Bond.
Description: Carbondale : Southern Illinois University Press, [2016] |
    Series: Crab Orchard Series in Poetry
Identifiers: LCCN 2016007914 | ISBN 9780809335329 (softcover :
    acid-free paper) | ISBN 9780809335336 (ebook)
Subjects: | BISAC: POETRY / American / General.
Classification: LCC PS3552.O5943 A6 2016b | DDC 811/.54—dc23
LC record available at http://lccn.loc.gov/2016007914

Printed on recycled paper. ♻

This paper meets the requirements of ANSI/NISO Z39.48-1992
(Permanence of Paper) ∞

Contents

Acknowledgments

I would like to thank the following publications in which these poems first appeared:

Adroit Journal	Kalliopē
Antioch Review	The Bells of Prague
Beloit Poetry Journal	Semper Fidelis
Birmingham Poetry Review	Bone Flute
Boston Review	Honey
Crab Orchard Review	Gold Bee
Cumberland River Review	Charon
Cutthroat	Ivory
Dialogist	The Invention of the Harp
Fiddlehead	*Prima Materia*
	Virtual
Georgia Review	Cello
Ignatian	Three
Kenyon Review	Wings
Laurel Review	Golden Ratio
Los Angeles Review of Books	The Progress
	Wind Machine
Luxembourg Review	Gift
New Welsh Review	The Paintings of the Chauvet Cave
Pilot Light	A Bridge Made of Water
Plume	Byzantium
	The Underground Railroad
Saint Katherine Review	The Invention of Polyphony
Southwest Review	The Invention of Paradise
32 Poems	Smetana
West Branch	Angel's Trumpet

Grateful acknowledgment is given to the *Crab Orchard Review* for selecting my poem "Gold Bee" as the recipient of the Richard Peterson Poetry Prize.

Gold Bee

Those in mourning know what it is

to occupy a space of great stillness,
an ideal that's never perfect for good

reason. It's ideal. Sealed in honey
like the sad bells and cathedrals of Prague.

I.

Kalliopē

Long ago a boy's harp had the power
to move stones, not far, but far enough,

to give the dull world the look of life.
Or so say the myths of men, long dead,

who, for all we know, never lied, but played
on their lyres and our desire to know.

Any rock will tell you, music blossoms
from things until, it seems, they are its source.

Who is to say they aren't, or one source
among the many. A harp asks a question,

and the stone's reply is never the stone's
alone. Nor the question. Conversation.

All of it. Tell me. Why do questions rise
at the end. Death, for one, turns to question

the underworld with a song that lifts
the frightened heart not far but far enough.

Some days music makes the better friend,
without the tiresome platitudes,

the false praise, the cold breath of heaven
that would tear the particular face

from grief. Once there was a beautiful boy
whose gift for song came from somewhere else.

True, we called his music his. It was.
And ours. You hear it in the difficult

hours his mother spent gathering the pieces
of his unconscious body. Stories say,

she kept the head, that part we imagine
was most his, that withered as hers alone.

Music is just one part of the story
that keeps departing and arriving, keeps

loss alive like an unanswered call.
The language before language, more quick

across the barricades of hell and nations,
the sound of names filled with nameless air.

When a boy plays his harp, a vein opens,
and while the harp does not understand,

it reveals. It honors the stranger that is
a lover or child, and so opens the puzzle

of embrace. Whose body is not torn
to pieces in time, whose time not the ardor

that music never masters but takes in
like this world's broken traveller or bread.

Who does not take their liberties. Let me
begin again, with her, the mother, whose name

some call immortal though we know better.
Long ago a god knelt in tender horror.

Nothing moved. Not far but far enough.
On the wind the blood oranges in bloom.

Cello

The final note of the prelude
in Bach's first suite pulls the oar

of the performer's bow closer
to her body, and so sends her

into the great black drift. Here
and there a calm where music breathes.

If the fall of rain were a still place,
it would be a song like this,

a long sizzle across the sea
that takes and takes and will not rise.

It would be the better version
of time, the better reason why

you follow into no-man's-land:
to see that hand about the dark

end that grips the bow's horizon
of hair, and think, when I grow up,

out of my body, I want a coffin
like this, a box on a spindle,

a warm voice between the legs
of a stranger who plays nothing

familiar until now. Long ago
the cello was my first glimpse

at what desire looks like—too
young to know the emptiness,

cradled and tuned, given shape
in spruce and maple and on rare

occasions willow, was my own,
the image of something missing

in me out there, and in a girl
I loved. But it was not love.

Who does not crave a little space,
an available motel or clean

bowl whose open mouth accepts
its thread of milk but never fills.

My first love was more a stranger
than I knew, and we fit together

well enough, image to image,
and my body floated out ahead,

some nights, into God knows where.
I saw beauty as form and not

experience, and the only home
of hope was memory on fire.

Perhaps I envied the cello,
its possible growl and coloratura,

how it might be either gender
and so the body of both

beast or angel and winter sky
and the hunger that survives the feast.

Those who travel heaven and hell
know the distance between them

could be the slightest adjustment
of the bow or modal cadence.

My second love was the deeper
wound, and I could not sleep,

and the streets at dawn were clean
as knives and glistening. I am

what I am not, says the cello
in love, not willow, not sound,

not these alone, not form even,
but the thin continuous dialogue

of freedoms other than our own.
Every word a conversation.

One could do worse than envy
a cello, to summon the dissonance

that draws you to it, the shiver
of maple, the pizzicato of rain.

Not the rain that falls, but rain
the moment that the falling ends,

the long cold thread to paradise
cut, and elsewhere, here, a voice.

The Invention of the Harp

The leanest sheep yield the toughest gut
and thus the strongest voice, the intestines

cleansed, extruded, bound into the dark
strings of harps that shiver, as storms do

and the closed eyes of animals that dream.
God knows what they see, if they hunger

for images of grass made of music, of wind
whose hand soothes with a gentle rustling.

Song began somewhere, we do know that,
and its voices tend to flock together

because they must, they want to continue
in each other, to survive as one

of the choir, to survive, as one, the choir.
The hungry are the most fierce, most alone,

long before they weaken from their hunger.
What they would not give to open up

the basilicas of mouths and swallow.
And the string made of gut remembers.

Even the blade that takes the lives of sheep
blazes the abject warmth of immersion,

the eyes that open when another's close.
Music knows. Departure is our calling,

our home, like the father's funeral a boy
dreams for years until that day it happens.

The cry you hear is not song, but it tears
now and then through the body of song.

The harpist grasps a chord and pulls it
into the air, but it is the gut that makes it

fly. The gut that lingers here, in the hand.
Hunger is always returning. Just what

it returns is, most days, a wordless thing.
But today there is a singing in it.

There again the silent music, the body
that opens its box of sparrows at dawn,

and the sun that is a harp on fire
sends shivers through the cold hard ground.

Bone Flute

Music's first instrument was everything
in the wind's path that made the sound called *wind*,
being elsewhere, summoned to the field
among the screams of reeds along the river.

Or some such thing we cannot quite believe
or disbelieve, since it makes no history,
and we, historians by nature, are always
late as those called *late* who came before us.

In this way we see in them the moment
we are in, the way music recalls its steps
to walk ahead, and there is no music
without that feeling of coming after, late

as archeologists in love with something
hollowed, and therefore made, by human nature
remade, a bird bone with four small holes
we take in hand and must imagine to see.

Ivory

As the unseen pianist begins to play,
light as the step to a sleeping child,

the spiritual that rises from its bed
of strings withholds from us the testament

of what it grieves or why, as if history
wandered out of its body, made less

factual, practical, wise, and yet profound
the way the depths of the Atlantic are

or ships that lie among the skeletons
of ivory and slaves. Music forgets.

That said, it gives the heart its reasons
to remember. Its reasons to forget.

Keys lose their warmth the way hands lose theirs
or the bereaved the first difficult hours.

Far from the shipwreck, a wave or two
unburdens against the shore. It grieves no one.

It loses its beauty to the inexorable
ache of decay. Which is to say, its beauty.

Once there was a man chained to his oar
who sang in time to the others. His music

recalled what a language in exile forgets.
Hopeless as a cure, and yet something

vital, quick to go where language can't,
his, or the unfamiliar others at their oars.

Back then each tusk came with a slave
traders bought to bear it from the jungle.

Most died. To every tusk, the lives of five.
Prices rose in kind to cover the damage.

Money is sensitive that way, like a sea
creature that is more tentacle than mind.

Or the machine of hands across the keys
that plays the notes that are no one's music.

Back then a man might feel all of Europe's
pianos in his pull. And in the song

that might have given him one last wind.
Say you stare at the ivories a while

and, being human, begin to wander seaward.
What you make out in the cream of scales

alone is neither major nor minor, but both,
depending where you start, where you end.

The home key, that is what they call it.
And everything else a middle passage.

The chanting of the chains becomes the part
you must imagine. Facts are dreams then.

They flesh the bones the way songs might flesh,
in turn, the facts. As the pianist wanders

without words, sent out in search of them,
he keeps passing over the *home note*.

No home really, more the long white tooth
of resolve that crumbles into music.

Or the breeze that maddens the flies in some
church basement in the Alabama heat,

that crowns joy and grief alike in diamonds
of sweat. Home as the afflicted eye

turned to ivory, the dark place that stares
through you, dead at the center you never

knew was there, and like it or not, you stare back.
And then it looks a little harder, farther.

The Invention of Polyphony

Then came the day a love song laid down
against the plainchant below, and yes,

the profanity of that ruffled the gold
feathers of men and angels in the loft.

But it was more than the *cupiditas*
of the human animal that stirred them.

It was the nature of entanglement,
the way one music pulled its needle through

the fabric of the other, to make of one
voluble scripture a medium of two.

It was as if there were two gods now,
albeit stitched in love's contrary motion,

and worse, the intervals between them
transgressed into the devil tones and close

discordance that longed to be resolved.
In censure lay confession, the unease

that heard its likeness in the urge to move,
the audible desire that takes two voices.

Still the pleasure of that kept bleeding
through the great cathedral doors with news

of a stranger music. The single-celled
creature of the choir wriggled into two,

four, eight voices, and the law it broke broke
down in some glad necessity of heartache.

What the hell. Invention is its own
law. God's seed fathers an anomaly

of twins whose ancient curse in time gives way
to the charity of mothers. They know,

the anima in the animal is made
to move like the breathing of one singer

into many. The many as the passage
of tension and release that gives birth.

What is an echo if not the child
of some other child. What a child

if not a little chaos, baptized in blood
that binds a body to all it would admit.

Smetana

When an ear creates its own private pitch,
its own cathedral-tone without clapper, bell,

or breath at the end that is the beauty of bells,
it is not music. It is desire stripped of its song,

the wire of its shield, the body of its deep sleep.
It is wind in the stationary trees of winter.

But say we take that note, that exhaustion turned
fever turned dawn of some impending deafness,

and hang it in the rafters of the string quartet.
It is not music. Nor is it alone. Discrete,

yes, and thus capable of yearning. Likewise
the man who watches a woman cradle her cello

with his suffering inside and hears nothing is
discrete, confined, afflicted, and capable of movement.

He is neither music, nor cello, nor broken body
alone, but in dialogue with those he cannot hear.

And among them, himself, not as he was or is,
but as he might be. As music is when it is passing.

Hero

Among the many styles of bereavement
and release, this one walks and therefore leads us,
not as a river or the otherwise stretched
signatures that pay our debts, but as one
strong hypnotic pulse drawn to the altar,
to the coffin hinge and the sky it opens.

Remember how the composer tore up
his dedication page, disillusioned,
how the *Bonaparte Symphony* became
the *Eroica* and thus a little lost,
flagged in anger like a house on fire.
But to hell with that, says the music.

We are alive, you and I, and walking,
the way a heart walks, over the unwritten
bar lines that stay unwritten as we go.
Who would not lie in music's river, still
and yet moving, moved. To think dejection
finds its equal there, among the reeds.

Or that the cradled violins preserve us
in memory without words, without, in time,
the memory. Only the will to have one.
When the last beat falls against its echo,
the record vinyl crackling into mist,
I feel old, refreshed, jittery as I lift

the floating needle, then lay it with care
in the darkened ring between the movements.
I too lie down in that black circle, listening
to the measures that would be personal
and not. Like the rocks we write on.
Or the trumpets of lilies that make no sound.

Say the dedication you lay in stone
fills with water. The elegiac movement
is not the name, but the rain that falls there.
One part of grief is always water. The rest:
exhortations, long tones, the low violas
who cannot tell you where they are. Or why.

Semper Fidelis

In a far room a child is listening to music
from the fabric on the hi-fi console

twice his size, no, three times, more, now
that there is music in it, and inside that,

the leafy crackle of vinyl beneath the needle
as if some beast were rummaging the trees.

If I tell you the child is me, it is me
as an enigma now, a speechless witness

just inches from the black fabric that is,
in turn, inches from a distant parade.

My father is away on business, and so
he takes the shape of records that he bought us,

or rather the family before I came
into the world, a stranger, though I must have

felt less of one, somewhere, far away.
The trombones are serious about getting

from here to there, and since I know them
as funny in cartoons, I hear their laughter

in a military number scored for horns.
It is November 1957,

and armies with their morning glories of brass
march our streets every Veterans Day,

me the glad hat on my father's head
and shoulders, bouncing in time because he bounced.

I still hear the trumpets' high sentence,
how they walk in time a flowered street

to reach their full crescendo as they pass.
Always America in songs and pledges

whose gratitude is too powerful
to be clear, like a boy's shadow

small inside his father's as it grows.
I do not quite know what people love

when they love their country, but for me
the music of affection begins with one

room, one face, one patriot, say, who
served on a warship in the Sea of Japan.

Mostly his stories go so far and then
trail off when things turn dreadful or boring.

Hard to tell. All I see is my father
before a photo of his destroyer drawn

across the shadow of the Golden Gate.
How patient his stare, a long time now

entering the ash-white fog in silence.
How small his body inside the visual

music of the harbor, the great wet chill
that flags the mast, the pallor of surrender.

Gift

Where there is breath, there is music
that mostly goes unnoticed. A light
broom sweeps the dust from our throats
and sweeps a little more back in,
so even as we speak we are giving
some measure back, some quiet rhythm
of quickening the world is made of.

Where there is breath, there is the voice
of oceans, the broken shore that flows
seaward as the sea withdraws.
And we feel refreshed, no matter
the particular discouragement,
bitterness even, the loss that curls
the body around its hands in bed.

One part keeps insisting on
exchange, as when the trumpet lends
the bass the solo, and the spot
drifts upstage against the darkness,
and what he plays is dark, a ballad
that smolders from the physical
depths. No matter the particular

light-beam that pools at his feet,
his shadow lengthens as it falls,
the way a tree falls into its shadow,
into those who listen, who must,
as if they did not know the grievous
beauty in them until they heard it,
out there, in ashes, and breathed it in.

II.

Prima Materia

And when I awoke,
the world said, let's be clear.
It confused me. *Clear,*
as in, out there, out lined.
Or the other notion:
clear as in transparent,
lens-of-the-spectacle
clear, tide-pool clear,
absolved of our refection.
On one side, the eye,
on the other the world
inside the eye. Confused.
And when I awoke,
an early sun opened
the ledger of the blinds
and said, let us be clear,
empty-wineglass clear.

Ask any alchemist.
Did he have mornings like this,
when he saw in the dreck
and vapors of the lab
the ghost of near things
becoming nearer, more
a blur. Ask him for me.
Why the weeping candle.
Steam, smoke, less than smoke, clear
as death to the dying,
birth to the unborn,
before the alchemy
of dawn torches the sky
to sublimate its angels,
the air's precious metal
invisible as a father's grief
the day his father dies.

Truth is, grief is lead,
however warm its plate
passed around the table.
Recalcitrant, crude,
impervious to reason,
it lays its worried burden
on the ocean floor
like a silent blessing.
But what do I know.
I am asking you, father.
What do I understand
of the bad heart you took
to the edge and back.
What you lost when you lost
your sleep. Why the clear
wind chime of the spoon
that fed you those black mornings.

I am asking the lemons
who raise their lamps in search
of you; I ask the winter
trees as they break out
in a sob of blossoms.
I ask the waves who bow
down and crash, eyes closed.
And the rain that falls
like a bride's black silk.
Or the rag of the night
custodian who clears
the slate, the one day's
dust of long division.
Let us be clear, it echoes,
as soil to the boot, boot
to soil, the harbor of Naples
to the spears of stars.

Let us be the star we see
in the one we do not,
pulled by the ghost force
of matter into matter
like a field of poppies
into the serum, the toll
of church bells into fog.
Earth calls each to lie
against the closed door there.
The end is clear, the earth
says, as in out there, out
lined. And yet transparent
as the glass-bottom boat
of a symphony at night,
as here and there, beneath us
where we sleep, the first
gold buds begin to rise.

The Paintings of the Chauvet Cave

Time was a man laid his hunted down
in a cave like this, cut open the fresh

steam of the body, and began to paint.
Look around. No human figures here.

Only horses, lions, a chimera, an owl.
Each an avatar, or so they would be,

each an infant hour we can't recall,
we who crawl on all fours to enter.

And for what. To breathe the inner chamber,
hear the voices that are no longer ours,

echoes that shatter batlike into silence.
If what you see are echoes, you are an echo's

echo, one more bison with all eight legs
caught in the stampede of the singular.

Time was a man wanted to be two,
four, eight such men, that, in the middle

of the night, longed to be one again.
Night bore down with its axe in the woods,

and the trees became a wilderness.
Ask the girl in convalescence who opens

a box of paints and feels a little better.
The same storm interrogates her window.

The same scavenger crawls from the hills.
The girl knows. When a hand lays a face

on death, it is not death. Only a face.
Not the beast of discouragement,

but the part that lives as the beast goes down.
These imitations, they begin in something.

These echoes return in a stranger voice.
Be calm, it says. Be watchful at the threshold.

Be thankful as the slaughtered shadows fall,
west to east, over the bloodstained wall.

Charon

When I took each coin
from his eye in payment,
I saw the minted eagle
pressed into the skin there,
its image laid so long,
first in silver, then flesh,
the lid too was coined,
and thus only a thing
of value when passed on,
as cells in life are passed
in trade for newer cells.

But this day, like any,
was unlike others, and
as I pierced the harbor
with my prow, he woke,
then stepped ashore to look
at the great white cliff,
his eyes too quick to see
the watery blink eyes need
to see, to know the world
we spin is winged in dark
and never seen again.

Honey

The light across a face has no face,
just as we have none in total darkness.
The light says, be calm, be vigilant,

be kind to those for whom eyes are cruel,
those whose look of misfortune begs
the question, do we look or look away.

They make of us a problem. They accuse
with their abjection as with their beauty.
They thaw their mittens in the sun. Light falls,

even tempered as honey, and so lies down
among the fallen. It is everywhere,
the unseen thing that makes things visible.

It consumes its flesh in a phoenix of dawn.
It eats into our rooms, and we, who eat it,
we hoard it for the journey. Look around.

A moth taps a window, and we think
it just wants to be let out when, who knows.
Sometimes you can want what you have.

A man grabs his chest in the orchard
and falls, and the wind is so sweet and careless
it seems to him the fruit has never been

this close, this nameless. Day's honey
stings, which is why we want more honey,
why we pour it into our darkened eyes.

And why not. I love so many men who fall
and cannot love me back, it gets old.
It gets me thinking of them the way a garden

thinks of the sun at night, how it rises
in its shoes of dirt and softly roars.
Light is new because it never is,

because it falls and falls just standing still.
It tells no story. It is the lamp behind
the story, the beam that falls beyond the film.

The moon knows. Or it becomes useful,
for some, as the face of one who knows,
the pool gone still to bring the sky to focus.

Truth is, it has a thousand faces, none
a moon. You can photograph them,
own them, pass them down for generations.

And what your children see when they look
is different from child to child. It is honey
in their hands. If my gods are personal,

if my fathers now and then are gods,
it is because the face that lies down
across the light of heaven teaches something

light alone cannot. I entered the world
through the portal of my mother's body,
through her gaze as she cupped my head

in one hand. Back then I filled that hand.
And when her face disappeared, the still
light of the empty room taught me how

to speak, to slip her name into the missing.
If my gods are personal, it is because
they never are, because I make them so.

Gods love a little maker. I believe that.
They love the little homes a day abandons
as it falls to sea with a star in its throat.

One face rises through another, suffused.
The new old mask eats into the younger,
but the eyes, they age a bit more slowly.

They are the child's flashlight in the woods,
the stranger in the strange dream, the sweet
nightmare where a man, a father, clutches

his heart beneath the orchard and looks up.
The sun has never been more particular,
more different from all other suns. Its face

looks down on earth the way a mother looks,
or a mother's absence. Somewhere a wind.
A stalk of corn rattles. And then it doesn't.

Somewhere a bee hovers among the lamps
of apples. Invisibly it blurs its wings,
this way, that, looking for an opening.

The Invention of Paradise

At first it did not work out so well.
All those expectations getting in
the way, like the thought of falling asleep
that keeps you up. The infinite applause
of fountains in the garden of delight,
it seemed a little annoying after a while.
Travel, after all, is not the same thing
as variety. The leaky tap will tell you.
And all those luxuries, and nothing but,
aren't they a little sad by human standards:
all that harping on this and the other.
Of course what we wanted was the soul
on better behavior, and heaven, though imperfect,
gave dark its stars, virtue its destination,
which, as bliss, was not quite virtuous.
But life was hard enough without the many
faces of dread hung high among the angels
or floating in lakes with planets at our back.
And then, it dawned on us, that paradise
might be less something else entirely,
that it has no gate, save the flesh we leave.
And what we glean from its imagined pleasures
is less its power over death than how
it lets death in. After all, the extremities
of joy were always the shadow play of shadows
and generous the way the heart might be
with sacrifice beyond coercion or greed,
more liberal with literal blood and emblems
of appeasement the moment it ceases to try.

Byzantium

Madonnas of the early church have no children,
only little men, the lean cheeks and mature

proportions of gods who neither weep nor smile
but look on as tiny fathers, eyes dark with calm.

Our Mother of Perpetual Help, she understands:
she who holds an odd small man, a king, whose hands,

no larger than a lizard's, ring her thumb as his
sole emblem of attachment. His gaze is elsewhere,

drawn aside to the severed body of an angel
with a cross. A bird would be distraction enough,

let alone a bird with a piece of the great wood
puzzle that makes men children and children men.

Do they save themselves a measure of mystery,
these infant gods. Are they merciful enough.

So many Christs among us—the African, the Greek,
the Flower Child—each the mirror of its culture,

a kind of pool we enter if only to disappear.
Here we see the mere space a man might go

if he could crawl back into the younger body,
into the sweet dark fat of the little terror

he was, powerless with wonder and lizard hands.
Take your own abandoned flesh. It taught you

like a mother who dies before you can remember,
so that her loss becomes the abstract grief you bear

or not, the ice-bright angel you can never know.
You were made to forget and so gild the hand

over the face of something that was more lustrous
with blood and the sting of being (when being was young).

Gold too is a thing of nature, as is the imperfect
art of forgetting. Remember the gods and mothers

who taught you to pare away the space around
each name. A gift, this art, the kind that would be given

like a cross from a skeptic to a believer in need.
The bright scarf of the stylized Madonna bears

one star of hope, one of fire, to grace in time
the many sickbeds of Europe and the New World.

If she holds fast her unaffected gaze, and he his,
born without a childhood, is he not the shadow

of men who live long enough to think it odd,
to wonder at the older consciousness of infants.

These gazes locked in precious metal, are they one
part comfort, the other the cold light of a day

long ago, a sunroom with a record machine
that plays the tune of everything we can't recall.

I try, becoming childish, small, and finally
phantom, clear as air that fills the child's cry.

The wisdom given a boy beyond understanding
asks, is there a wisdom other than understanding,

other than suffering. Can it be the difficult summons
of suffering, yes, but lowered in the odd dark

well of a sympathetic eye. Can it be a kinder,
darker heaven, this life, a less childish friendship

beneath the cross, in the airborne radiance
passed invisibly between us. Like coins in a bowl.

Midas

My life savings are my picture
of old age as it spends what's left,
the last dollar, the final breath
I never draw, for it's the gold
bird whose song is a still place
that will not die, the sweet unheard
as heavens are and graves and all
they take, hold, and cannot touch.

The Underground Railroad

And then I found myself inside the subway,
in an abandoned hall that smelled of smoke

and metal, whatever it was engines breathed
that blew the glass doors open and closed.

And somewhere in the corner of my eye,
a man sat in his weary shoes and blanket,

his fingers inside his beard as he ate
a piece of paper with *sandwich* written on it.

I know. There are things here I cannot see.
Who am I to ask you to believe

the way a nightmare believes its point of view.
Which was always more of a field really,

where people are not quite people anymore.
They are the word *people*, and I eat them

the way tunnels eat the trains that leave us.
I drink them with the instinctual relish

that drank from our mothers once, that gave them
back their language in a strange new tongue.

Say we weep the dry tears of paper and pen.
They are not ours alone. Once I touched a man

with a dollar that was my fee to enter
a world where no one was me or not me.

You and I, we meet a lot of people
with our eyes closed as if we were listening

with care to the music in their voices.
Empathy was always one part music,

the other a traveller waiting for a train.
Morning breaks, and the subway darkens.

So many voices everywhere they blind me
to their mouths. Still I walk this thoroughfare,

this common chamber as it gives and takes
and feels nothing but acts, yes, it moves

like money changing hands, or tough talk
picked up on the way. It gets things done.

God knows the lengths a man in need will go,
the stretch of hunger that draws a body out.

My ignorance takes the shape of that man.
He is dark, deep as the passage before us,

the exhumed well lying on its side.
There are always more particular faces

to mint the coin of the human eye,
more shadows drowned a pool of shadows.

There are bodies that stare into the hole
at the end of the landing, all of us

eating the tiny sugars of our bloodstream.
When a train blows out of the word *train*,

our shoes shiver in a crescendo of light.
Doors sigh, inhaling. I check my pocket

for my wallet. I make myself small.
And the roar of the tunnel takes us in.

Three

My last wish, my disadvantaged nation,
my empty room in a childless marriage,
you of all numbers understand the odd

and lonely margins, how the holy ghost
feels among men who get the lion's share
of press. You, the white behind the scripture.

The one hand claps like a bell that calls
the one from the two, the two from one.
And you, the stillness of the third that listens.

Say I am here, what I think about there,
and you, the spirit where it happens, nowhere
in particular. You are the light of thought.

Play something soulful, says hell to the boy
who will not be consoled. And as he leaves,
sworn never to turn to see what he desires,

his singing braids a ligature between them.
You, my friend, *are* that music, that trembling
in the leaves. She is really there, you tell him.

Earth here, autumn there, and you the air
that touches both their faces. What is a face now
if not the shroud of daylight laid upon us.

What is the gift of speech if not flowers
on a face's grave. The sun's axe splits
day from night, and a red ache binds them.

And when the leaves fall, you are the falling.
And when the wind beats a flock of crows
to cries and tatters, you are the silence after.

Golden Ratio

It's in there, the fetal curl of the sea
in the shell. And the cochlea that hears it

fold, whitened under its own design.
And though the pattern collapses into shore,

the ocean keeps insisting on another,
drawn to what we understand to see.

*

The golden ratio has no water in it,
no Vitruvian posture, no animate

sunflower with its vertigo of seeds,
though it provides a language, not for one,

but for the many in the thought of one.
Not the blossom, but the blossoming.

*

Gold as the siren's call in the fog
of the physical, pleasure's rectangle

that frames the eye, the lips, the first teen crush
cut from a magazine. Gold the choice

that singles out the rare that would choose us
in return. The many in the thought of one.

*

To choose and be chosen is to be one
small gold breathing machine in the arms

of another. Long ago I was nameless,
and then one of a kind, and then both

and neither, and I lay my puzzled head
on a girl's chest in the silence after.

*

The gold rush of the mathematical eye
sees what it desires most everywhere,

in the helix of genes if you look hard
enough, zero in, make the connections.

Or in the mineshaft of the eye in eyes
it sees, loves, then does not see, then sees

*

more clearly. The abstract angel is no
evening in Kansas beneath the chirping crickets.

Let alone the girl I knew there. Gold
measures on the radio and in her ear,

they had no girl in them although I heard them,
incorruptible as angels, passing.

*

Satie wanted a music that counted out
beats in gold ratios among the portions,

his *Sonneries for the Rose-Cross* a mine-
field of seeds that petal when you touch them.

Gold as the first Rosicrucians imagined:
as the coming together of blooms and crosses.

*

Rose: the sexed ephemera of weddings
and funerals. Cross: the pin that goes

through them like a gold-plated number.
Oh, do not be so boring, says the music.

Beautiful, as mindless acts of kindness,
passing: singular and therefore nothing.

*

That girl and her radio keep shaking
off their principles. They are the youth

that gold frames. Eternity the headache
of some better tune. I once saw desire

as a piano whose hollow place would float it.
Then as the overflow in a bed of strings.

*

Satie knows. A light hand fills a room
with emptiness. The glasswork of voices

gives us the water to clarify our thirst.
Numbers that sing to one another, once

they were nameless, then a gash, pulled
through a cloud where the sunlight flowers.

*

The gold ratio of the crucifix
takes its measurements from one man.

You can go mad with the tiny nails
and hammers that pin a world together.

But something suffers. A man turned gold dies.
And then the stories. Changing. Into songs.

*

Where there is no God, there is always
her double. By design, the echo chamber

gives a sky in movies the voice of wells.
Satie knew the stitch of counterpoint

understands less than it knows. The gold
rose is only as good as it imagines.

*

It is neither rose nor dead. But unborn.
Like the death of a child in the singing

that a mother cannot bring herself to join.
It is hot in the chapel. Flies in the windows.

A candle weeps. It centers everything
for now. Most gold where the wax burns down.

III.

A Bridge Made of Water

The figure on our horizon is no metaphor.
It is a man on a bridge overlooking the Los Angeles River.

River might be a metaphor, depending on the season.
For it is summer, and the shine has dwindled

to a trickle in the whiteness of our page.
The sun in the water is no pearl. And no sooner

we have placed a pearl inside the sun.
We cannot help it. We transgress. Like a river.

*

Pearls drizzle downward through the bloodstream
of the man who searches the river for the sky there.

Standing water comforts no one. Nothing
like rain, a nerve of light running through the gutter.

The sound of a river is another word for stillness.
Another city to grip its thin blue threads.

Any wonder we cling to our waters long after
the trappers and scouts float seaward in canoes.

*

The history of a city is written in rivers
that would bind us the way blood binds

a body to the ocean it crawled out of,
the one that kneels into a hissing of sand.

History as cryptography reads backward
into the tide's obscurities of music. It makes,

on us, a claim. The power of city over cities
downstream. Written in the history of rivers:

*

water as the life-vein of dominion,
the precondition of give and take and take again,

water as the commodity that floats
all others, that enters the city bearing

thin gray clouds of factories and ashes.
But water knows no dominion. It knows us,

say the passages it writes, the figures we use
to note the space between us. The birds.

*

One half of every metaphor is knowing,
the other the unburdening of what we know,

the surge in the slash of understanding.
The old rivers are out there, somewhere,

impatient to carve a cold script
across the warmth of our aging look.

Flesh that holds like death to small
and smaller freedoms as the bed grows large.

*

Any wonder a face in Los Angeles
keeps turning to the face in the impoverished stream,

turning to, and into, turning one face
toward the many, and the water rises.

One and one and the many ways we have
to record the river one grows small in.

One above the flowing coffin of rain.
This funeral music is never ours. As ours

*

is not. Cities on maps bend lazily
into parks and memorials that unravel the likes of us.

Hair comes undone in the dark car
parked against the shoulder that swells and falls.

And the green-lit music from the dash
pours through the children who listen

better in the dark, their eyes opening
and closing, the river gathering water as it goes.

*

Say a man at a desk is closing up
for the night, his memory of numbers

still flowing downward in his eyes,
figures water-fallen to the black sea

with a hidden music, a rhythm
of pulses: one foot and then another, alone,

down the long stairwell, one, one,
as if one alone would bear him onward.

*

Say a man, obsessed, lies down in a river
of numbers and one begins to seem like two

as never was or will be. Not like this.
And the child he was in the coffin

of a silent room could be any child.
The wine in him turns to blood, to water.

To leaves turned away in the wind.
To speak one word for leaves and wind.

*

Night rain throws a net of calm
over the sleeping child, and we have all been that child,

eager to become the one we have never been.
One half of a figure must be the given. The other,

the made, the wilderness of rain. No, the man
in this river is not a river. He's a guy, more real

than he imagines. And so he looks down
from this bridge to find his image looking back.

*

Is it true, we rinse our eyes in each night
in the currency of darkness. All across Los Angeles,

the quiet violence of the new. Men do
what they do. They pass on. Their bodies are rivers

that flood the banks of those they leave behind.
No, the man on the bridge is no metaphor

And so his summons to become one. To bow
at the corpse like a breaker that will not fall.

*

A word that clings to the stillness of paper.
And in it still the water crumples.

The widow weakens at the knees and someone
younger holds her by the arm. It's like this,

says the sermon: a storm gathers,
and God is calling his children in.

As if we took our names with us.
Or the name would pull us from the other side.

*

My first laughter had a little terror in it,
a little relief. Boo. And a door of hands

opened. A face appeared. Nothing is funny
without distortion. Funny-weird, funny-ha-ha.

Bells charm in the distance. This much is clear.
The time they measure is a bridge in flames.

Try falling in love with a world that never lies.
Never burns. Bells that toll. These are facts.

*

These the cryptography between the towers,
their numerical postures of plain stone.

It's like this. We are no one. Then helpless.
Then similar to one, similar to no one. Long ago

I came here. Where the Los Angeles River
meets the sea. The rise, the crumple, the phosphor.

From the Greek, *phos*, for light, *pherein*, to bear.
Long ago I came here with my father.

*

I knelt like an ocean to trace my face
in the water with a stick. This is one way

to destroy a face. To honor it. Nature holds
a mirror to art the way death holds a mirror

to our nature. I hate death. And love the fruit
it bears. This mirror, this light, this bridge

made of water. These exhalations *borne*
across the threshold of this, our native tongue.

IV.

Gold Bee

Invention is the mother of invention,
and so the bee coated in gold, arrested

in flight, pays homage to the lens that sees it,
to the microscope of the new century

that made this gilt a necessary thing.
For gold loves an electron, carries it

along the bloodless vein of the wing,
thrilled in stillness, to make a sharper image.

What then are these electrons if not bee-
bound for the hungry flower of the eye.

A bee like that is everywhere you want
to be: everywhere the whir of wings

that halo the hidden violence of attraction.
If this is one more music of the spheres,

it goes unheard because we always hear it.
Like those first few months when we were tiny.

The eye too is a haloed thing, an angel
gilded in the light of foreign objects

that come and go, and the eye burns on.
Likewise the meadows that are the mother

of bees who give, in turn, birth to meadows
that pull at heaven and earth to be seen.

Their corruption is everywhere, as blooms
that pay the boatman to ferry their gold away.

Or so says the thrum of petals no one
hears, the blurred wings of ghost essentials

we coat in the flown colors of spring.
Can you blame us if we sweep the floor

of bees and sing to see them fly a little.
Those in mourning know what it is

to occupy a space of great stillness,
an ideal that's never perfect for good

reason. It's ideal. Sealed in honey
like the sad bells and cathedrals of Prague.

Or the pharaoh's coffin glazed in metal
for the journey. Gold dreams the long dream

of an underworld economy.
It would stabilize the terms of give

and take, the forces of impoverishment
and fortune that litter meadows in their season.

Nature envelops nature and calls it new
as death is new and violent and still and never

still enough. If you look hard there,
you can always see something moving.

It is your eye looking hard, moving in.
In as in the word *invention*: *in venire*,

an entering. Always a child inside us,
grown small, a steeple and the thread of day,

poorly remembered, that passes through.
Inside every memory there is another,

a place that waits with the patience of heaven.
Always a speck of dust, quick as music,

and made things that would make the maker.
They're in there, the powers of invention

that open something: the bee the blossom, the blossom
the eye, the eye the bee-gold eye of bee.

Tooth

Being small, you plant a tooth
beneath your pillow and feel it

bite into the soft place below.
It is the lantern that leads you

into a basement of lost things—
a puppet, a friend, a reason to weep—

and with its light makes the odd
less odd in their solitude,

their separateness that binds them.
But you, you are more alone

than you know, still, given over
to the company of good things

that speak low and turn to money.
Young enough to lose a tooth,

old enough to hide it, you tell
no one and so find no quarter

in the morning. Only a kernel
of bone. Dead as silver pretends

it cannot be. Until it leaves you.
Your disappointment is not

the cash night promised to exchange.
The residue of sleep is always

drying between you and the dead
castoffs of you. Money is always

turning into money, teeth teeth,
the body the intricate machine

it cannot be. Until it leaves you.
Everything has changed. And nothing

is yours, which is to say yours
alone. Teeth fall like tiny gears,

and it takes losing them to know
you are elsewhere, as old suns are

with their hoarded silver of lake
and star, when night was none the wiser.

The Progress

If you sit still, you can hear it, the thrum
of the power cables that puzzle a sky

grown intricate with satellites, doors,
hands that write the checks to make them open.

It was always this way, not the cables
but how a puzzle loves a harder puzzle,

the cell an animal, the beast a town.
Long ago my mother taught me to be

hungry, to pry the shutter on our piano
that carried the tune she always longed to play.

If you sit still, you can hear it, the clock
among the millions who grow old with us,

who sit beside radios and gold frames,
snapshots of the kids when towns were small.

Long ago progress was a river
fed by snows that never ceased to fall.

The bombs we invented we would invent
into extinction. So said the music

in my teacher's voice. I loved her. I listened.
I hid beneath my desk from history's

strange devices and the will to use them.
But the sky is different when we are small.

A bolder, more manic blue. Long ago
I laid my hands down, ambitious to play

a piece to fill the emptiness of ambition.
Always a city inside the city, rising,

complicating its traffic like a tax code
or circuit board that makes hands obsolete.

I met a man once who feeds the homeless
of Los Angeles. It's complicated, he said.

They break the law to live now, they must.
In other words, the law is broken, shattered

into the numberless financial concerns
that move their eyesores further into hiding.

Which says, I live in many cities. In one,
the smoke of factories and oil drums.

In another, a mother's love that tells me
how to hide, to hunker in the basement

when the missiles fall. So simple then,
we thought our sunglasses would make a difference.

Or that hope might repossess the anthem
in our hands. If you sit still, the room goes dark,

the world more articulate with stars,
with the flashlights of phones that screen our calls.

Music is everywhere we aren't these days.
And yet it touches us, we cannot help it,

the child's hope that feels a little hopeless.
It moves to move us, snowing in elevators,

spilling through the windows we cannot open,
in fallen light of which, we will, we will.

Virtual

When we speak the word "life," it must be understood
we are not referring to life as we know it from its surface of fact,
but to that fragile, fluctuating center which forms never reach.
                                                    —Antoine Artaud

From the Latin *vir* for *man*, and beyond
that the embattled connotations of *virtue*
as manly, and thus with valor, force, strength
implicit in the cardinal summons to men
of good character; we have come to this:

to the word *virtual* as we know it, move it,
use it to call what worlds are when we world them,
or the lakes of mirrors that flood the eye,
that lay kids to waste beneath their goggles,
in a morphine of larks whose silence is song.

Virtually impossible, we say
when we admit some dire measure of chance,
our proximity to nowhere. Such is life
beneath a star where life looks back in turn.
Well, not really of course, and then we see it.

Virtual, meaning *almost*, and therefore far
enough from somewhere to power the theater
of cruelty or heaven or some such calling.
If we animate the dead, who can blame us.
They too have needs, virtual mouths that speak.

They too have something missing like machines
that talk to guide us, friend us, over the phone.
The modern air so full of phantom wires,
hard to tell the connected from the confused
who yak out loud to their beleaguered angels.

I am talking to you and seeing a stranger,
Antoine as an old man, his bony jaw
striking out like a ship into open seas.
I want to say I understand when I don't,
how it feels to shiver in a hospital

in southern France as the world you knew
is everywhere and lost. I want to arrive
here: in Rodez, city of medieval iron,
of whores and tulips the color of cardinals.
Beauty is surgery. I do know that.

Sure, the voices he suffered that were not there,
he loved them once. Cruel, histrionic,
alive, they were the body that breaks to feed
the many pigeons of the churchyard. His cast,
or one such cast that fluttered with the scenery.

But if it's true, that theater is the stuff
of matter turning into mind, whose mind is it
really. *La réalité virtuelle*, he called it,
when he was younger, as was his suffering.
Imagine if the virtual forms reached

the human heart out there in the world
where life is and death and heaven's floodlight
on the stage of earth. Surely the ghost
we cast over our eyes is ours and must be
strange and fragile as the oldest of men.

As power fades, its fantasy increases
in valor and madness, however fortunate
or not. Memory takes on the virtual edge
of tulips in winter. I am talking to you,
Rodez and the cathedral on your shoulders.

And you, the past, I see you. I am talking
to the bladed camera of the petals.
So red I can almost touch you, charity
that opens the blush of these maternal fields.
Vir as in the virile stem crowned in blood.

If facts could dream, they would be a feast
like this. They would be the lonely machine
that almost listens as it speaks. Almost
suffers the fire of the mirage that floats
ships south. And dies at dusk for no man.

Wind Machine

I do not know her, the woman caught
in the passions of the wind machine
as the cameras work their angles,

her hair blown back to imitate the spirit
of youth and whatever they are selling.
I do not know her, but I love her hair,

the way it moves about in the stillness
of the photo, the bedroom tangle just so.
Must be something in the look of speed,

the illusion of approach, that keeps
hands flipping the pages to feel the breeze.
But we know better. If winds could pass

out or wither from exhaustion, it's here,
in fashion pages glazed as cakes and fast
cars that men afford when they are old.

We know the wind is not the paper it blows
any more than breath is flesh, flesh a wind
machine we take apart and reassemble.

I do not know the woman or her product,
though I like to think she is paying off
her student loans, and the gaze she wears

she has borrowed from a man, a stranger
with a long lens, who whispers, yes, yes.
What I do know is the wind is real wind,

sweeping back and forth from some machine
that says, no, to the camera's little death,
the blades of the shutter, the capture of souls.

Who has not had a troubled love affair
with stillness and walked the galleries filled
with dead and beautiful things and felt renewed.

You hear a lot when the world goes still.
Just you and the portrait of the woman
with her sick child who, if lucky, died old,

possessed by spirits such as yours. And then,
you are that child. You are the wind
in the lungs of the child and ask your mother,

is she afraid of death, and she whispers,
no. Her hand is in your hair. *It's nothing*,
she says. And then, more softly, *nothing, nothing.*

Wings

The movies have fallen in love with the machine
again, with the voice of the telephone

inside the phone, the ghost that would be dead
and alive and ours to cradle in our palms.

The movies are lonely, and so go out
to the movies, in love with the dark

and vaulted ceilings that could be starless
heaven in this light. The machines are lonely,

say the angels in *Wings of Desire*,
lovers who long for the otherworld

of blood and silver, refrigerators that beg
for coins in motel halls, red and glowing.

They call out at the modern screenings,
no beam of light above us, no angel dust

that clips the shine and rises through the story.
The merely visible is the new unseen,

like stuff you own and long to own again,
quick to tap the finger that taps the link,

because, Christ, it is lonely in this sky
full of starlets that skeleton our eyes.

Machines have fallen in love with love
that bores itself to death, as if death

might die the way it does in the movies
and great cathedrals, whose heroes rise again.

The lavish cathedrals adorned with fetishes
of torture, they too are dead and generous

with empty space, the air that is a friend
to those whose angels are never people

alone and never apart. The movie idols
who can't break character, they must be vacant

somewhere in there, inside the circuit board
that is synaptic as sex, love, and the space

between, the part in dreams that is not dream.
What is light without the invisible

space it passes through, without the spirit
of a felt idea coming into being.

Complexity is the new gothic, the angels
in the lonely house, the phone that talks.

They must be vaulted with a higher will
and echoes that articulate new things

no voice has told them, phantom songs that matter
because they are new, a.k.a. alive.

The great machines of theaters and chapels
must know what it is to feel abandoned

and have a choice, to be alone, like money
that makes the kind of money machines can make.

Cities that grow grow toward greater and greater
complexity, the starry circuit boards

we see in the lonely mirrors of movies,
when the starlet falls in love with all

she sees, out there on the dark horizon.
Dead gorgeous, this distance, this rain forest

of light that took a million years to arrive,
as machines arrive, to guide us on our journey.

In a world where machines are people,
what do people become. What the lonely

science that promises to live on as those
who lived it die the death the starlet dies.

The new theaters are chapels and chapels
theaters that miracle a knowledge

to raise their shine so high against the skyline.
They must be empty to be glorious

and full of desperate promise that is the song
of thought. They must torch the path they take

in thought, like song. Like song's technician
at his machine, they must be generous

with what they have not done, what they endow
to choice after choice. This our paradise

of choices that angel the dark, our great machine
we sing into that makes our voices large.

Angel's Trumpet

Horror movies made for children tell them,
go ahead, laugh, you are on the threshold
of greater disbelief, where nothing is worse
than the dolor of clocks that loose their tension.
The dead are alive at least. And calling.

Not unlike the *angel's trumpet*, the downward
drooping flower that poisons adolescents
with delusions, the whole burnt orange choir
flared, tendrilled, darkest at the opening,
there in the parkland, just south of school.

It does what once the dead in movies did,
the ones whose eyes were strangely distant, slow,
their pupils swollen with the earth they came from.
No pride, no conscience. Even as you eat
the leaves that eat you, it bears no malice.

You could be opening your car door,
lifting your head from a desk at the same time.
Not that either is dread, but both might be.
Faith is your worst friend now. Your night prayer
where hands seek each other like a mirror.

Naturally you hate to lose the surge
of blossoms on your tongue, but your body
knows some blood sugar needs to be expelled.
These angels that pour their music through,
they say, *where everything is real, nothing*

is angelic. For though your friends shake you,
call you, it is your voice alone in them.
Your throat in another's halo of bone.

The theater bolts its door. The movie begins.

Gold

The complexity of the gold flute is one
part music, the other what it says to us

who hear its look and scarcity, what we
want in the lust and luster of the metal,

the lure of the lamp-lit curtain seen
from a distance by a boy in the street.

Gold is made of distance, of the held
dissonance that would keep promising

an end, but cannot end and keep its promise.
A gold flute is one part money, longing

to spend its last breath elsewhere, in the arms
of a dying fall that comforts us to tears.

*

If music were a thing we hold, we could
end there and find it a little irritating,

like the willfully obscure with nothing
at stake. People knock themselves out

for the more beautiful story with them
inside (and outside at the same time).

And say the couple there consummates
the truce between them and the emptiness

that leads a body like water to a glass.
Gold is both the emptiness and the filling,

both the body and the day it seizes.
The pocket of change and its little chime,

they can make you hungry with music
like a grand choir of empty mouths.

Scarce but not too scarce, gold makes its coin
an angel, its angel a coin, a good faith

covenant that there is more to desire.
This shine of the mirror makes it larger.

*

The illusion of that, larger still.
At a certain age I knew. I wanted

to get close to the loveliness that scared me.
She had a name I made particular

at a distance and I wanted to break
something, I was just that happy sometimes.

I was cast in gold, though I could not
see it. And music minted in awkward joy

would become the youthful thing that lingered
as I aged. Oiled vinyl in tattered sleeves.

If heaven is money for those who believe it,
so is ignorance. At a certain age.

The gilt bird and its real song have this
in common. They comfort us in exchange

for what they disturb. If the rarest
flutes are the warmest, we just might feel that

in the bush on fire that won't go out.
Or gold that is the dead and sexual child

among the metals, the first to seize us
with captured light, the last to corrode.

*

If Artephius (alchemy's holy father
alive in us as rumor and song) burned

a hole in night to find *it*, it was youth
he wanted, sure, but possessed by spirits

older, more refined, selective, wise.
He wanted to be the child of his search,

particular as love is when it chooses one,
whose name it labors to make personal.

Mercury, lead, cobalt, rust, the wind
and fathomless dark of Athens, the ruffle

of trash and branches that breaks one night in two:
to each its name that is the girlfriend

of the world in the distance, veined in gold.
Particular and so longing to be more

a part. Gold as the cornfield of heaven
we harvest and plow and harvest and sometimes

there is a little singing to make work light.
All of nature under the alchemist's fire.

Even gold can aspire to be more gold
or, like angels, labor to be common.

Back then truth was an aesthetic and often
elsewhere, like a blood-red terror that clocks us

in the morning, the real as promising
more than this, these sheets, damp with sweat.

*

Gold was the signature of the center
that was everywhere, and seeing was its

author. Holy things are expensive.
It makes them harder to find, harder

for them who look for us as the child
who looks for kindness in sex, sex in kindness.

A monstrance is polished with the love
that choses and so leaves a portion to dark.

The interiors of nature are always dark.
And certain wisdoms tinker at the vault

of matter for what it never fully explains
Gold becomes a language for certain sex

as the language of returning to something
changed by fire. What we ache our lives for

is too often what is young and sinking
into pleasure we find, no sooner, sinking.

*

Artephius sketched an abstract of faith
that loved rocks as the flutist loves her flute

because of where it takes her and being
the reason why. Gold as the bird of fire,

the angel's signature and so a pretext
for the burning of men like Artephius.

Gold as the language that longed for a tongue.
He even ate it. Which is what a kid

would do. Or a painting that is tasteless.
Or a song that fawns over the girlfriend

of its own taste. But songs that would be true
alone are no less childish and pissed off

at the phonies. We need a kid like that
in a certain age, as the lead complexion

needs blood, or an aesthetic of ugliness
needs a better reason to fall in love.

We need a kid full of vinegar and piss
the color of gold. J. D. Salinger wrote

to an age like that, and he burnished
each word in his novel to a natural gloss.

To be particular is to listen as love
is particular and then complex, called

to forgiveness, less choosy as it goes.
Gold kills. And we cloak our angels in it.

*

Who does not live with the dissonance
that holds (too long) their gods and precious items.

The final city has a gate and, one hopes,
a better reason to be kind, to burn holy

objects by the light of their own fire.
The flute knows. Although it never asks.

Sex too, at a certain age, needs a better
reason, and shooting galleries a better

connection, the dreary parks of Wichita
a gallery on the river with a Hopper

in a gold frame. The old friends are lonely.
Keep them, says the doggerel of youth.

And the austere beauty of the portico
in New England that settles no argument.

It is the music in the expensive throat
that is warmed by gold but has no gold

inside it. No. It loves the commonplace
refined to be more bare than we remember:

the great press of sunlight on a window,
the face whose eyes have the long acquainted

look of exclusion and invitation
like doors that open into empty rooms.

*

At a certain age, ignorance is butter.
And then it is ignorance. And over.

The distance between a painting and the heart
it touches, it is not permanent. It is

an emblem. Not gold, but the illusion
that makes the mirror of the painting larger,

as bodies are, when we pass through them.
Once, the painting says, I was a boy

with a flute for a heart, and the wooded
lot behind our house a place a girl's name

was so particular it was the angel
of the particular. Once I made her

laugh with my mistakes. They are out
there, says the solitude of the plain

and beautiful face that never changes.
They are opening with laughter still:

the mouths, the buttons, the final puzzle of her
small gold latch that held our shadows in.

The Bells of Prague

The day Charles the Fourth died, the bells
of the royal cathedral began to toll
without a man to toll them. So goes the story
made of many stories. A man dies
and a widow writes a message in bronze
to share the thing that leaves its bronze behind.
A man dies and the great stone faces blanch
in a host of pigeons. What a city carves,
it scars. The ardent couplets turned to stone
lie still beneath benedictions of smoke
and frost, coal pulled by ship up the river.
So can you blame a story if it grows
beneath the breath of factories at dawn.
A king dies. And the many belfries
of Prague toll in kind without a man
to toll them. Not grief. Alone. But mourning.
A reverie of howls that sweep the yards.
This love of kings is someone else's story
still. A fable sugared with snow and ermine.
Which is why the ecstasy of bereavement
keeps moving out, looking for a listener,
taking, in someone, its final liberties.
You must admit: the chime of ice that brittles
is beautiful. Its bells are gods that die
and die again. They make ghosts of metal.
Just as words, laid in bronze, would be.
Discords hung in the great stone carriage.
When a man dies, a girl sings at the table.
It happens still. And everyone stops to listen.
And sometimes there is a hush that follows,
a space that honors what is past and passing.
And sometimes, the voice of a great expansion,
each heart moved to stillness. Like a bell.

Other Books in the Crab Orchard Series in Poetry